Casper - A Short Tale abou[t]
B[y]

Copyright © 2013 Brenda Armstrong

All rights reserved. Except as permitted under the U.S. Copyright Act of 1976, no part of this publication may be reproduced, distributed, or transmitted in any form or by any means, or stored in a database or retrieval system, without the prior written permission of the publisher.

Dedication

To all my friends old and new who love Casper and my Casper stories and to those who encouraged me to write about him.

Thank you to Casper's Fan Club for requesting updates on him.

A very special Thank you to my husband for saying "let's give him a try" that first day we saw Casper. For your patience when my mind is in a "writer's zone", and for never doubting for a minute that I could write this book.

To my baby dog Casper, the sweetest, most loving little fur baby I have ever had the pleasure of caring for, I love you!

And last but not least to my grandchildren, Coby, Jocelyn, Morgan, and little Craig Jr. always remember you can be whatever you want to be in life but most important be happy.

Table of Contents

Dedication

Preface

Chapter 1	*Lethal White*	2
Chapter 2	*Don't Be Afraid*	4
Chapter 3	*Doggie Love*	6
Chapter 4	*God and Dog*	8
Chapter 5	*Does He Know?*	9
Chapter 6	*The Adoption*	10
Chapter 7	*Home Alone*	14
Chapter 8	*It's Time*	16
Chapter 9	*Art of Humping*	18
Chapter 10	*Loss*	21
Chapter 11	*Bird Dog*	25
Chapter 12	*First Words*	28
Chapter 13	*Paw Sign*	29
Chapter 14	*Sixth Sense*	31
Chapter 15	*Life is Good*	33
Chapter 16	*Run Free*	35
Chapter 17	*Road Block*	37
Chapter 18	*All He Needs is Love*	39

PREFACE

This is my story of a tiny two pound special puppy that has given so much joy, love and humor to my life. Casper was diagnosed at eight weeks old first as an Albino then later as a Lethal White. I am no expert on both subjects and what I know about the lethal white gene I have researched on the Internet or from discussions with various veterinarians.

Casper doesn't act any different than most dogs and he looks like any other dachshund except for the fact he is white. His eyes are a little small because he is blind; Casper is also deaf. Yes he was born deaf and blind.

If you were to see Casper out on a walk he would appear to be as normal as any dog, however, he does have some special needs. Special needs may not be the correct term but he is indeed very "special" and some of his judgment "needs" a little help now and then. Being blind along with not hearing can be a little challenging and dangerous especially if he is outside. This is why I call Casper my special needs baby; and I know how to provide him with these needs.

Imagine a pup in the womb for weeks then once it is born the world is still silent and dark and nothing to guide him but his sense of smell.

From the first day he became my little fur boy he required months and in some areas years of patience and understanding. Most of all he required lots of love and closeness.

Looking back on his first three years if I could have spent more time with Casper I would have learned his means of communication much sooner. In his early years I worked full time and missed a lot of the important signs but he still grew and learned a great deal from just our love, patience and consistency.

My husband Charley and I tried many different ways of teaching him and ourselves what it was exactly that he needed from us besides our love. Early on we decided to simply teach him according to what he was, deaf and blind.

I tried to imagine what it would be like to not be able to see or hear only smell. To a dog that depends strictly on his person or persons to care for him it had to have been frustrating. But for Casper, he trusted us completely from day one. I believe he sensed the love we had for him. He was and still is such a loving and happy little guy, he is truly amazing. He doesn't know a world of light or sound. He doesn't know how cruel the world can be to defenseless creatures. He doesn't know that he is deaf and blind. How would he know? Never seeing or hearing, darkness and silence is normal for him. There is no vanity involved nor does he suffer from depression. He knows nothing but the loving touch of a human hand.

From the time Casper was a baby dog he used his nose to navigate. Today we joke about him never growing into his nose and how God must have made it extra-long to help him get around. It really isn't that big it just seems more dominate because of his white coat and black nose.

During our training of Casper hitting or swatting was never in our program of teaching. The first year by far was the most difficult but we used a lot of love, tenderness, consistency and a whole lot of patience.

Housebreaking Casper was very easy. In fact he was the smartest pup I have ever potty trained. When it came to his chewing and biting however, he bit constantly! Chewing and biting or mouthing as it's called, is normal for a baby puppy as they are teething. For Casper it was not only teething but his form of communication. And communicate he did very well; I have the scars to prove it! After many attempts we broke him of "teething" on our skin by holding our thumb gently and firmly down on his lower teeth and turned his attention to a toy or chew bone.

When it comes to puppy love I am very opinionated. In some of the following chapters you may not agree with my tactics and that's ok. It worked for me and I am just sharing my story with all you dog lovers. I truly feel after you read this book you will understand why this very special little puppy grew from a tiny fur ball into a very loving, independent little man.

I often cringe to think what might have happened to him or what kind of character he would have today if he would have been raised by the wrong people. This little guy could have ended up a vicious biter or worse in an abusive home if the owner lost his patience. A forceful or "I am the boss" type of mind set would not have worked with Casper. We used consistency, kindness and love.

Casper is my eighth dachshund. I loved them all very much but, Casper is definitely my special one. I hope this book brings as much pleasure to you, the reader, as Casper has brought to me. I think you will be amazed at how limited his challenges are today.

Chapter 1 *Lethal White*

Casper is a white, blind and deaf dachshund. In medical terms he has been diagnosed as a lethal white. The term "Lethal White" is a name used because of the lethal gene he inherited at conception.

Years ago humans would kill white animals for fear they would be deaf and/or blind. Lethal whites come about from the inner breeding of all the wrong colors in animals. It's all about the genes. You can research about Lethal Whites on the Internet. In nature this cannot be prevented but in the case of humans breeding dogs it can. All it takes is an amateur breeder taking a chance by breeding the male and female that has the wrong colored gene pool before researching the outcome. (I must state that I am being polite).

Some of the pups are just lucky the others are "defective". I have read that years ago some breeders just got rid of the defective pups, but in our case when we heard about this white little dachshund we had to see him. The minute I saw him, it was love at first sight, he needed to be in our family.

Many books advise us that these genetic oversights can survive in a loving, caring home, I am proof. Lethal whites often after their first year develop other problems such as: heart, liver, respiratory etc., or their immune system can be compromised. So far my little guy at the age of 5 years is healthy and so very happy. He just can't see or hear. We lucked out in a weird sort of way. Maybe he was just incorrectly diagnosed, because he is very healthy, happy and content.

Imagine a nine inch long, two pound baby dog with white shiny hair as soft as velvet, the softest pink tummy, a black nose with a little pink spot on it, blue eyes and little pink and black paw pads. So beautiful in his own little silent world! He just needed closeness and love. His color and markings so unique and so was he.

8 weeks new (Weight 2 lbs.)

Chapter 2 *Don't Be Afraid*

This book is about Casper. Because I am his Mommy I thought you would be interested in my background which may explain my soft heart for this little guy. I hope you will bear with me for just a couple of chapters before we get to Casper's story.

For many years I have noted a small number of people who are afraid to look or talk to any person that appears to be different looking. I call it ignorance which actually is not a demeaning term. It simply means "lack of knowledge".

Remembering back to my childhood I was afraid of different looking kids or adults. I remember seeing a boy in our town with pure white hair and pink eyes and he scared me because he looked different. I recall asking my parents why he looked that way and they explained to me he was an Albino and the word scared me. Being a child I was (of course) ignorant to the term Albino the meaning and how genes control the way we look.

My baby dog Casper also gets those looks. Ironically the majority of the looks are from adults not children. If we are out and about some adults will glance at him frown and pass by without even coming close to him. A true dog lover is different. A dog lover will stop and can plainly see he is blind by looking at his eyes. The dog lover will then pet Casper and let him give them kisses. A true blue dog lover will let him lick them right on their lips! Casper's new fan and I will usually discuss the fact that this was a genetic disorder from birth and what a sweet little guy he is. At this point in our conversation the person has already noticed how friendly Casper is.

Children will rush over and ask to pet Casper. He has already smelled the child five minutes prior to them seeing him. I always agree to let a child pet Casper. He absolutely loves children! I believe he senses their innocence the minute he smells them. He loves everyone actually. But as most dogs do, Casper has an extra sense as to who likes him and who doesn't and he won't even wag his tail if he smells the later of the two.

Over the past 5 years I immediately explain to the new admirer that Casper was born deaf and blind. This tends to shorten questions and gives me more time to run my errands.

Since my husband and I adopted Casper, friends have listened to my stories about our little guy (usually funny stories) and would tell me I needed to write a book about some of our little fur boy's actions. I started to keep notes about Casper over 4 years ago, somewhat like a person keeps a baby book on one of their children. One day I started adding the stories to my PC and to my surprise, I had enough notes to write this book. I really felt a deep need to share my experiences, fun stories and the progress of this tiny pup in hopes it will encourage others not to be afraid to take on a pet with a handicap. They are truly amazing! You do have to commit your time, patience and lots of love to the animal or it will not work. These animals are very special and have to be treated as such.

Chapter 3 *Doggie Love*

I have always treated my dogs with a tender touch. My children and grandchildren were raised showing nothing but respect and love toward their pets.

Doggie love is something I learned as a little girl. It took years for me to realize just how intelligent dogs really are and their effect on humans.

As children my sister and I were never without a pet. Wiener dogs, a cat or two, a horse and my sister loved lizards, turtles and chameleons. I personally preferred dogs and cats myself. Our dogs were pretty much limited to dachshunds until in our teens my sister's boyfriend gave her a German Shepard mix pup. She needed a lot more attention that we could give. I think my sister had to find a new home after the pup ate our Dad's good cardigan right off the clothes line.

Our first pet was a wiener dog (dachshund) and her name was Penny. I just recently learned from our Mom the reason for her name was my sister and I used our savings of pennies to purchase her. Penny was with us for fifteen years. I myself was 20 years young and I saw her fall over to her death (which I didn't know at the time) and ran to tell my Mom. She immediately knew what had happened. Later that day my Dad had to bury our Penny and many, many tears were shed for the sweet little girl.

Years ago my Aunt cared for my sister and I while our mother worked outside the home. My aunt had 6 dogs at one time and a cat or two. She talked to her pets just as though they were little children. We use to think she was "a little off in the upper story", but soon the love for the animals became second nature for us.

At times our Aunt would hand feed one of the cats after it coughed up a fur ball. She was always giving one of the cats some kind of medicine that smelled really gross, I think it was an Iron supplement. The event that sticks out in my mind for some reason is when the much dreaded Vet visit was approaching for one of the dogs! Yes the big infamous spay or neuter visit. My Aunt would start fretting 2 weeks before and wouldn't stop until her baby was home after the surgery. As a kid I didn't understand what the big deal was but once I became a doggy Mom myself I totally got it.

Chapter 4 *God and Dog*

We all know that God spelled backwards is Dog! How perfect is that! Whoever named our closest friend was no dummy that's for sure.

Have you ever really thought about the coincidence? I have many times thought deeply about it. Who besides God loves us unconditionally? Who is always there for us no matter what mood we are in? Never criticizing or cursing us and always listens. God loves us all and forgives us no matter what. God is always listening when you need him to listen. So therefore this all makes total sense, who besides God and your dog are always there when you are in need? Never judging, cursing, or belittling you when you are down. Yep it's God and also your dog!

Your dog gives you loves and licks when you are down and waits patiently for your return when you leave. He will lick your tears, wounds and your smelly feet. I mean really I love my husband but I won't even do that for him.

I have a sign hanging in my family room that reads, "God help me be the person my dog thinks I am"! I don't know who wrote the phrase but we should all think about it and work on our character and souls.

Let's face it there aren't too many people that enjoy putting up with a moody human, except for "man's (or woman's) best friend"! Under all conditions our dog loves us! Yes indeed God and our Dog!

Chapter 5 *Does He Know*

I am not sure I can break the news to him! He is such a love how am I going to tell my little boy that he's a D-O-G? I am not crazy and I am sure a lot of you treat your fur babies better than some people treat their children. Casper has always received the best care available. He has never been allowed to go outside in the winter without his sweater on. He can't stay out in the summer sun to long for fear of sunburn. He is our child and is treated as such. I ask you how do I break the news and say to him, "Casper, my sweet little four legged boy, you are a D-O-G"! My husband and I have discussed that maybe he already knows because his food and water are placed on the floor and he goes potty outside! Who's to say?

He may get the slightest little hint because when we leave the house his bed moves to the laundry room. I make it very comfortable for him fully equipped with his bed, blanket, toy, food, water and air conditioned or heated. But I still think he may wonder. He doesn't seem to mind (the laundry room) in fact he likes the security of the room and his bed when we are gone.

What really amazes me is he knows when we are leaving! I have tried many different ways of preparing to leave the house but to date I can't figure it out. He just knows. He will go into the laundry room and sit and wait until I move his bed in the comfort zone. Of course he gets a treat. One of his doggie treats divided into four (4) bites! Yes Casper can count, I am sure. And if any other item besides a treat is given to him when I leave he freaks!

One day I accidentally gave Casper a chew bone instead of his normal treat (divided into four bites) and he flipped out! He barked and whined and I couldn't figure out what was wrong with him. After a few minutes I realized he related a chew bone to going to bed and I am sure he thought I was putting him in the laundry room to go to sleep for the night all alone! Casper sleeps in the bed with Mommy and Daddy not in the laundry room. I removed the chew bone replaced it with his treat (4 bites) and he was just fine. He knew the routine and I screwed up!

Chapter 6 *The Adoption*

It was an October morning and I was busy at work when a co-worker called my desk and announced there was a lady outside the reception area asking for me. She also told me this lady had a baby puppy with her. Knowing my love for dogs, and what a soft heart I have for dachshunds she had come to my workplace. In her arms this precious, innocent baby pup. I reached for him and he immediately snuggled to my neck and lifted his head and he gave me loving licks on my mouth. I looked into those beautiful little tiny blue eyes that could not see me and all my "motherly instincts" or empty nester hormones came to life, and it was love at first sight.

I called my husband who worked nearby and described the little guy to him. Although we had discussed many times (no more fur babies) our Schnitzel (also a dachshund) was the last dog we would have until we retired. We felt it unfair to any pup to be left alone all day and if we decide to take a vacation we didn't want to worry about finding the perfect doggie sitter (if there was such a thing). Need I say more? My husband drove over to my place of work during his lunch time and held the small defenseless creature that licked him also. I expected an immediate NO! My husband looked at me and (I know after smelling the puppy breath) said "let's think about it today and sleep on it".

All day I mentally fought with myself. Yes, no, Yes, no, not another dog. Schnitzel would be so upset being the spoiled "only dog" that she was. I called my husband after about 2 hours and he said let's give him a try until Sunday, (it was then Tuesday), if it's too much we will take him back. We also made the decision to have our veterinarian take a look at him after work the next day.

We drove to the breeder's home after work and picked him up, the minute I had him in my arms I knew I could never let him go.

During the ride home he fussed of course and when we arrived home and introduced him to Schnitzel she sniffed then tried to pick him up like a toy! Schnitzel understood "no" very well and backed off. I then proceeded to feed him, love and rock him in my arms and sang to him. He loved it and settled down and went to sleep. I then placed him very carefully into a hand me down bed with a previously worn t-shirt of mine. He slept all night. Dang! How easy was that? An 8 week old pup sleeping through the night! Geez that was easier than when I had my human babies!

Needless to say having just adopted a new baby dog the next day I dreaded leaving the little guy alone in the bathroom by himself. I wasn't quite sure how our Schnitzel would do all day with him but I felt he was safer alone than with his grumpy old sister. So the bathroom it was. I seriously even considered staying home but decided to put my big girl underpants on and go to work.

Of course I made sure he had a warm place to sleep, newspapers to potty on, food, water and the t-shirt that smelled like me! He did fine, but me that's another story. The first 2 days I left him home I swore I could smell him on my clothing at work. It was like a mother leaving her baby human after 6 weeks of maternity leave. I seriously could smell a baby dog (which smelled like baby powder to me) all day! I couldn't wait to get home at night. It was torture until I got home and saw he survived and I smelled him.

Since the adoption was on Tuesday, I had 3 more days of work until I could spend all day with him on Saturday and Sunday. I made an appointment with our veterinarian for Wednesday evening after work to have our little boy checked over.

That evening the vet confirmed Casper was truly blind! But to our surprise he was also deaf! We were devastated to say the least and sickened at the thought of giving him up. What would become of this little guy? He would need extra love and attention and patience that only "we" could provide.

The vet advised if we kept him it would be like having the "Helen Keller of dogs" and a huge undertaking on our part. The Vet asked that we let him know if we decided not to keep him, and that he would completely understand our decision. He also advised that a lot of these dogs cannot be trained nor do they live much longer than a year old.

Our veterinarian also advised that the problems of a Lethal White can go beyond being blind and deaf. He went on to explain the other health problems he could have (such as heart, liver, respiratory, compromised immune system, even pressure behind the eyeballs and eventually the possible removal of his eyeballs.

My husband and I seriously cried all the way home for the little guy. Casper was such a sweet, innocent little guy we knew we had to keep him no matter what. He needed to be in our care, our home, and we vowed to give him all the love and security he needed until he became ill. If it were only for one year, two years, three years, or however long or short of time we had with him we promised to care for him until the end.

Casper slept all night for weeks alone in his little doggie bed in the bathroom and we continued keeping the two dogs separated during the day because I wasn't one hundred percent sure that Schnitzel would tolerate his biting and jumping during the long days were we at work. Casper had as most pups do his wild play time and of course sometimes an older dog doesn't have the patience for pup play. Each evening when we returned from work Casper had done really well during the day alone. He also remained very cozy at night alone in his little bed.

At approximately 12 weeks old I put him down for the night and tucked him in his little bed and as always I shut the bathroom door and was expecting to relax and go to sleep. All of a sudden he charged the door with the power of a pit bull and he literally started "yelping and screaming". That was the end of Casper sleeping alone. I guess he was tired of being separated one more night from his people. Enough was enough for him and he was going to sleep with his parents!

I soon forgot what it was like after a tiring day at work, to just chill out! I didn't have a sound night's sleep for about 2 years or any down time in the evenings. I will be the first admit "yes I had second thoughts" but the thoughts only lasted for a few minutes.

For those of you that have had puppies in your middle age, it is the same as having babies at an older age it's much easier if you are young. I compare Casper sleeping with me to having a furry piranha in bed. I went to work for weeks looking as though I had encountered a gang of bougainvillea shrubs and lost. Those baby teeth were like little razor blades. I understood the need of him needing to burn off the puppy energy so I took a doggie toy to bed nightly and we would play for about an hour. Casper would get the toy in his mouth and swing it around until the toy would fall off the bed (and I got to fetch it each time)! I would fetch he would chew a few minutes then drop the toy on the floor, I would fetch and so on. He was training me! Finally, I resigned to purchasing a braided rawhide chew. What a life saver that was for my little Helen Keller of dogs and for me.

Three Months Young

Chapter 7 *Home Alone*

As weeks progressed Casper did exceptionally well in the bathroom alone daily. He still insisted on sleeping in the bed with us at night. We continued to toy with the idea of putting him and Schnitzel in together during the day to help shorten the hours they had to be left alone. Each time we discussed it I always found a reason not to. Until one very memorable evening (Casper was 12 weeks old). We had just got home from work and I went to save my little guy from the bathroom in which he had spent alone all day. I like to call this Casper "HOME ALONE"!

Upon entering the bathroom I found his doggie bed was completely destroyed and the stuffing everywhere. Doggie crunchies mixed with water, newspapers, and toys more stuffing everywhere. How could this tiny, innocent blind, deaf baby dog create such a mess? My husband reminded me that Casper had been the only one in the bathroom the entire day so, "he did do it"! After an hour of cleaning up we decided he needed some company, even if it was an old dog with little patience for a pup. So the decision was made, but how were we going to break the news to Schnitzel?

We purposely went out to dinner that night so we could test their companionship. We decided on a restaurant close to our house so the maximum time would be just short of two hours. It worked! Yes, no blood he was still alive! Schnitzel, (if dogs can) gave us a real disgusted look. She was beyond being put out! Her little face looked at me as though to say, "Well, I hope you had a great time"!

The next morning Casper was left in the care of his elderly sister Schnitzel. They actually did well together in the hallway on a daily basis. They each had their own little beds, (one pink and one blue) and often Casper would be in her pink bed curled up beside her when we arrived home in the evenings. The hallway had ceramic tile and once in a while we'd come home to a mess but not very often. Schnitzel I must say looked a little rough around the edges some days, but she survived. She did, however, insist on sitting on her Daddy's lap as far away as possible from Casper for the rest of the evening.

Home Alone

Chapter 8 It's Time

As every dog owner faces around four months of age, it was time to set up the much dreaded sterilization appointment. In Casper's case the "neutering" appointment. My baby undergoing the knife! My blind and deaf baby boy!

I was very concerned how he would feel in a strange antiseptic environment without his Mommy. I knew it was a necessary procedure to prolong his life (even if we didn't know how long that would be). It would also avoid complications that male dogs get when they are older. So I made the phone call and the appointment and talked with the receptionist about my concern. In Casper's case I wasn't worried about the actual procedure. I was apprehensive due to him being deaf and blind and alone in a strange place in a cage

Can you imagine the scent that a dog picks up in the Vets office? And with Casper having such a keen sense of smell (due to not hearing or seeing) he would smell fear, sickness and perhaps even death. I requested they do his surgery first so at least he would be sleepy the rest of the day until we picked him up after work.

I followed the normal procedure of removing any food or water after midnight which was not a big deal for him. I dropped him off, hungry, at 7:15 a.m. that Friday morning for his big event. I handed the Vet tech my worn t-shirt and his blanket (so he would know I wasn't far away). I made it to work on time at 8 a.m. and the first chance I had I called to check on his recovery. I seriously thought about taking a family sick day from work that day. I was so concerned that he would be fretting wondering if I would ever return. I now understood why years ago my Aunt made such a fuss!

I must say that was one long day for me but Casper came through with flying colors and didn't even need an E-Collar to protect him from licking his stitches. We received a lot of kisses when we rescued him from the Vet's office and Casper acted as though nothing had happened to him. We were off for the weekend and I had the chance to spend extra time with my little guy. And to this day he has never missed "the boys".

Chapter 9 *Art to Humping*

In my experience as a dog owner I believe most dogs hump! I have also had many friends tell me their dogs hump. Male or female they hump. I have witnessed this myself and my feeling is there is an art to humping! I have seen dogs hump a person's leg, (child or adult) they don't care. Dogs will hump their toy, their bed another dog's toy or bed. Some say it's a dominance thing, or it's because they like the object they are humping. Whether it be a person or an object there is no embarrassment on the dog's part. Now Casper he definitely shows an art when it comes to "humping"! For him it's a form of entertainment and exercise. He's bored!

In the beginning of his artsy pastime, his humping was narrowed down to one single bed and it was his sister (Schnitzel's) pink bed, not "his" blue bed. Well we knew he didn't know what color it was so it had to be a friendly, You know the kind of I'm so excited, I love my sister, please play with me sort of behavior. He would physically push and pull the bed all over the room, nibble and flea bite it, hump it, bite again and so on. He had a constant routine in the way he humped her bed. I really think he just wanted to play and she was a stick in the mud when it came to play, so he played with her bed because he loved her.

Since I am on the subject of humping the most peculiar thing happened one morning to Casper. I recall it was a Saturday; otherwise my husband and I wouldn't have been enjoying a fresh cup of coffee and just hanging out watching the dogs play. We noticed Schnitzel had returned back to her bed and of course we always kept tabs on Casper's whereabouts! Our little Casper was running around wanting to play with someone anyone or anything.

Casper had just turned 5 months old (in human years I don't know what age that would be) but whatever the age he was definitely going through the "penis discovery" stage! My Son went through it at the age of two (but never to the point I am about to describe). When my son was a little guy he always wanted to accompany the guest to the bathroom if and only they answered yes to the question, "Do you have a penis"? Quite embarrassing at the time! He shortly got over it!

Casper had been playing with one of the doggie beds, pushing, pulling and flea biting all around the family room. This particular morning I was watching him very carefully because a few days before he had grabbed ahold of one of my beautiful spider plants and pulled it to the floor. So as I was watching him Casper had this huge alien looking thing that resembled a raw turkey neck (but much larger) hanging out of his belly! It was huge! The fact it was so large I just knew his little body couldn't handle such a huge thing! I let out a scream to my husband to take a look at that "thing"! It was gigantic!!! My husband (looking from a distance) screamed back at me, "it must be part of his intestines, quick, hurry call the Vet".

Being a woman the last thing I was going to do was call and be transferred to a male veterinarian. I refused just knowing I was going to get a male on the other end of the phone. And how was I going to diplomatically describe this huge alienated turkey neck appendage hanging from the middle of my baby dogs' tummy? Meantime my husband and I are still arguing as to which one of us was going to make the phone call. As I disappear to get the spray bottle of water from the laundry room my husband called the vet's office. He was transferred to a female vet on call! LOL

The "thing" was still hanging out of Casper and even affected the way he walked! Kind of like a fifth leg (but much longer)! My husband proceeded to describe the problem Casper was having and also the fact that he had been neutered about a month prior. As he continued his discussion I started spraying the "alien" with cold water! I had it figured out now where it was coming from. I recalled my Aunt using the outdoor water hose on her male dogs when they were violating the females! The cold water didn't work. I ran to the first aid box and grabbed Vaseline, OMG! That was really scary and I really didn't want to "touch" it! But I could tell it was hurting him! He was just so tiny and this "appendage" that was sticking out was at least 10 inches long! Keep in mind the little guys' legs were only about 4 inches off the ground.

My husband had since got off the phone and advised me exactly what the Vet had told him. Back off, (no water, no Vaseline) and "it" would go back where it came from. He also stated the Vet's advice was that the possibility of it happening again was great. Needless to say I was beside myself when I found out my precious little baby dog had just experienced an erection!

Talk about sex education! I had never heard of such a thing! But as the old saying goes you learn something new every day! To this day I still think about that alien thing sneaking out of my puppy and also suspect our story to be one of the funniest moments of her career for the Vet on call that day. Also, for the record, the alien has never appeared since. We also have moved and along with the move came acquiring a new Veterinarian. Thank Goodness!

Chapter 10 *Loss*

    To lose a fur baby is like losing a part of your family, it's tragic! Our pets depend on us to feed, bath, and love and protect them, they are our children. Not only do they give us unconditional love, but so much companionship. Our pets are only with us for such a very short time.

    I think it's the same for most of us once they start aging. In the back of your mind you know that day will come when God calls them to doggie heaven but you can't imagine them not being by your side forever. It's such a difficult time but if a dog has been ill I think we reconcile to the loss much better than if it happens suddenly.

    Our little Schnitzel was almost thirteen years old and I could tell she was showing the normal signs of aging. She was slowing down and seemed less flexible during her walks. At only thirteen we really thought she still had a few years left in this world. Schnitzel was overweight and I blame myself for that. We didn't walk daily and should have. There is a quote I have heard many times: "if your dog is overweight you're not getting enough exercise." I did take her for walks but as she aged the walks became shorter. And during the Arizona summers the heat was sometimes just too much even in the evenings.

    For the rest of my life I will always remember June 11, 2011. And the time was exactly 5:15 p.m.

    Our granddaughter, Morgan, had arrived earlier in the day from Reno to visit for few weeks during the summer. Morgan and Schnitzel basically grew up together. There was a bond like no other when it came to Schnitzel and her human girl Morgan.

    From the time Morgan started walking she would pick Schnitzel up and sit her gently in her dolly stroller and off they would go through the house. If anyone but Morgan tried to put Schnitzel in the stroller she would jump right out. We taught Morgan to be very gentle with Schnitzel and as Morgan got older she understood the importance of just how gentle she needed to be.

I compared Schnitzel to a baby doll and Morgan understood. We never just turned her loose we always supervised their play.

Over the years as Morgan and Schnitzel grew they learned to swim together. We had our pool built in such a way that a very short legged dog could jump up and out onto the deck. There was a large island type structure at the shallow end of our pool that allowed the grandkids, adults and pets to sit in about 4 inches of water and relax or get out of the sun if necessary.

On this day of June 11, 2011, I had just arrived home from picking Morgan up from the airport. It was a very hot day as June days can be in Arizona and Morgan wanted to swim right away. As always she talked Schnitzel into a swim. They got in the water carefully as they had for years and Morgan let Schnitzel go about 3 ft. from the island. Schnitzel swam to the island and jumped out! They continued the routine a couple of times.

The heat was stifling so I let Schnitzel sit for a while in the shade and wrapped her in a towel (it was way too warm to be all wrapped up) but Schnitzel always liked the extra warmth if she was in the shade). I noticed that Schnitzel was panting and decided to put her in the house knowing she would go lie down on her bed.

About a half hour later I went into the house to refresh our cold drinks and Schnitzel was still panting. I knew she couldn't still be hot so I carried her outside just in case she had to go potty and she did. I returned her to her bed in the house and I went back outside to join my granddaughter. We swam for about another half an hour.

Upon entering the house again I noticed Schnitzel was still panting. I carried her outside and we sat for a while on the shaded patio and Schnitzel let out a cough. Water ran out of her nose and mouth and I noticed blood in the water. I put her down very carefully on the deck and she took one step, collapsed on her side and closed her eyes. I was so shocked I couldn't move. Within seconds she started panting again and opened her eyes. I remember praying to myself, "God, please don't take her now". (Her Daddy was out of town).

I knew I had to be strong for Morgan but as hard as I tried not to, I started to cry. I suddenly remembered a book I had just finished reading about the purpose that a dog brings to our lives. I told Schnitzel what a good dog baby she had been to all of us as I dialed our veterinarian.

The office was closed! We wrapped little Schnitzel in a dry beach towel and we headed for the emergency vet clinic 15 minutes away.

As I drove on the freeway the West sun was shining directly into my tear filled eyes. I continued driving with my eyes pouring tears and Morgan sitting next to me in the front passenger seat holding Schnitzel. We were only about eight minutes from the exit to the vet's office when Morgan advised that Schnitzel was gone. I glanced over and sure enough those beautiful brown eyes were no longer sparkling. Morgan then asked me to close Schnitzel's eyes. I reached over with my right hand and closed my baby's eyes.

The Emergency vet was wonderful. The minute we walked into the office a technician was there and she took Schnitzel out of my arms. I remember asking the Vet tech if she could confirm that Schnitzel had passed away. The assistant verified indeed that she was gone and asked if we would like a print of her paw. Of course I said yes and within minutes she presented me with a sweet little print of our baby's paw and also her body in a card board box so I could return her home.

I wasn't sure if I wanted to bury her in the backyard or have her cremated and I didn't want to ask my husband nor break the news that she was gone during a phone call. I took our baby home for the night and the next morning, drove Schnitzel to our local Vet and Morgan was by my side. The office was only open for emergencies (as it was a Sunday), so I dropped Schnitzel off for cremation the next morning. When I picked up her ashes on Monday, her regular Vet brought them to me and expressed his deepest sympathy. We later learned that congestive heart failure is what took our little Schnitzel and she was sure to go very soon as it was. It was almost like she waited just long enough to say goodbye to Morgan, her best friend.

Morgan volunteered to stay up and tell her Grandpa (Schnitzel's human Daddy the news and she did. We all mourned for days but it seemed to be a lot harder on my husband, perhaps because he didn't get to say goodbye.

I left Schnitzel's little pink bed out (per the advice of the Veterinarian) so Casper could have his mourning time also. His way of mourning the loss of his sister was to just lie in her bed. We moved a week later and decided the wisest decision was not to put her bed down in the new house so I packed it up damp with my tears. Once we arrived at the new house I only put down Casper's bed and he didn't seem to mind. He knew his sister was gone. It took him about a month then he resumed his ceremonial happy humping time, this time with his bed.

Schnitzel and Casper 4 months old

Chapter 11 Bird Dog

In our geographical area of Arizona during June and July the water in a swimming pool is somewhere between eighty to ninety degrees. It's a perfect time for a pup to swim especially a dachshund (as they seem to be a little more cold blooded than other canines). Plus a dog's normal temperature is warmer than a humans is.

As I mentioned previously our pool was constructed to be pet and child friendly. My husband and I didn't introduce Casper to the water until he was around nine to ten months old. We didn't want to scare him and wanted his first swim to be a pleasant and comfortable experience. When the water temperature hit about eight-five degrees we took Casper out to swim with us one evening.

Due to the fact Casper couldn't see or hear we were not going to take anything for granted and decided to take extra care in introducing him to a very large body of water. I held Casper very close to my body as I got into the water. My husband and I stood facing each other about three feet apart. Like dummies we expected Casper to swim to one of us and we would catch him, return him to the water and head him in the opposite direction to be caught again and repeat the three foot swim back to the other person; didn't happen!

Casper could swim, he was a natural. But time after time he would swim in different directions, sometimes to the right and sometimes to the left and often in a circle. In water there was no way for him to navigate like he could on a solid surface. He apparently couldn't smell as well in the water. How silly we felt and after thinking it over for a while I decided it would sort of be like someone dumping us in the middle of the ocean at dark, blindfolded and our ears plugged. It made perfect sense and I felt really terrible for scaring Casper. He didn't seem too bothered and I write that off to his dedicated trust in us. He had a nice refreshing swim and from then on we always held him in the pool and made the decision not let him outside around the pool alone.

We continued watching Casper carefully around the pool and one of us always sat where we could see him. He had the back yard memorized so well that I seriously didn't worry about him if I was outside. He actually got so confident when he was in the backyard he would run; play and walk really fast right up to the pool's edge and come to a screeching halt! He smelled the water I guess? On some days he apparently felt so brave he would stick his nose down almost touching the water.

There were times I would notice him following me when I was out by the pool. He would bravely be right behind me like a little shadow. I recall one December morning I was out checking on my plants and Casper was walking just a little too fast. Instead of him paying attention to his sniffer he walked right off the edge of the pool into the deep end. There was enough of an outward curve on the edge of the pool and he had become so confident but that day he had a whoops, he fell in. I scooped him up and dried him off (the water was about 50 degrees at that time of year) but he was fine. He was actually more than fine. He jumped, turned circles in the air, jumped again and ran and jumped right into the fountain grass next to the pool. It was the funniest sight. White wiener dog thinks he's a bird nesting. He loved to get wet and lie upon the nest!

One warm day during the summer I was outside watering and the pups were with me just lounging in the sun. I ran in to the house for just a split second to answer the phone. At the very moment I answered the phone I heard a scream from the pool. I mean literally a scream! It was Casper! He had fallen in the pool and was frantically pawing the edge to get out! He was only 2 feet from the safety step. I fished him out dried him off and he coughed and coughed up water! I was terrified but he was so excited he ran around like a kid getting off the best ride in the amusement park and proceeded to jump back into the fountain grass and roost like a little hen.

I made a trip the local pet store that day and purchased a life vest for Casper. We put him the pool and he did well with it on but still had no way of finding the safety step! Thereafter, each time I put the life vest on him (before we went outside) would cough as though he had water in his lungs and he was in the house! Crazy "smart" little guy! Talk about "conditioning"! And the end of that story was he never fell in the pool again after I invested $40 in the life vest. Go figure! Soon after we built a new house "without" a pool and moved.

Chapter 12 *First Word*

When it comes to barking Casper didn't bark until he was over two years young. I attributed this to the fact he had never heard a bark. Schnitzel was still with us when Casper was two years old and the little mini that she was, she made up for two dogs. She barked at everything, the door slamming to the neighbor's car, a person walking down the street, a mouse two blocks away, if Schnitzel heard it she barked! My husband and I had discussed we were actually lucky that Casper wasn't cursed with the "little dog syndrome"

One evening the dogs and I were relaxing on the sofa watching the news as we waited for my husband to get home from work. Casper was on my lap and Schnitzel right beside me on the sofa. Schnitzel let out a bark (she had heard my husband pull into the driveway). OMG! Casper must have felt the vibration and he let out the deepest, loudest AARF I had ever heard! Not a bark, but an AARF that literally hurt my eardrums! My boy had just "AARFED" his first word!

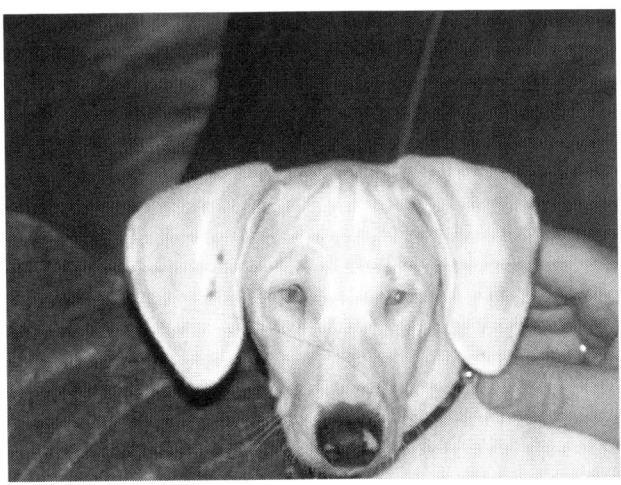

Casper age 4 months

Chapter 13 *Paw Sign*

I have found that my Casper behaves much like a small child. I remember back to when my human children were around the independent age of three to four years, they just wanted to know Mommy was near.

My children were always busy doing something as most children are. If one of the neighbor kids wasn't over to play then my kids would entertain themselves for hours! But just about every hour or so they would call out my name, find me, and give me a hug or just say hi, then off they would go back to what they were doing. They just needed the security of knowing Mom was close.

It seems customary to me that our fur babies need the same attention and affirmation from us as our human babies did or do. By the time Casper was three years old I soon began to notice how consistent his habits were with mine. He had learned my routine quickly and knew exactly what time I stopped and sat down to relax. In fact at exactly three p.m. every day, to date if I am not settled on the sofa next to him, he sits in front of the sofa and waits for me. He knows no matter what I will be watching the T.V. (Monday through Friday) because The Ellen DeGeneres Show starts at three p.m. I watch Ellen and Casper gets extra ear, back and neck rubs. Someday I hope to share Casper's story with her as I know Ellen is an animal lover also.

Casper and I have developed a very close bond since I retired. He lets me know when he wants to be held, by jumping up at my legs. I hold him for a while and then he's off exploring again.

For the past year and a half he has learned how to speak (what I like to call) "Paw Sign". He uses his right paw and "paws" at us. If he is beside us or lying in the bed next to us he uses his paw sign. Whether it be a milk bone, glass of water, (yes he has a cup of water on the nightstand) a toy he has dropped or to go outside he is adamant about his paw signing! And if we don't answer to the one paw he uses both paws!

Casper is very insistent when he wants outside if he is just hanging out inside the house. He uses his paw at the patio door and if we don't notice he will bark until someone lets him out to do what he wants or needs to do. Sometimes when I let him out he will turn back to smell if I am behind him. If I am he will run right over to the outdoor swing. He loves to lie on the swing with me next to him. He loves the motion.

There are times in the morning hours I will sit on the swing with him and I will read and he will snooze on the swing. At times he becomes so relaxed he will actually let me pick him up and hold his head against my shoulder while I rock him. This usually lasts about 30 seconds. When it comes to being held I am positive he has ADHD, his attention span is very, very short and always has been. But wow, how precious that 30 seconds of bonding is to me.

In addition to understanding his "paw" language. I have trained him to understand ours. A pat under his tummy means go potty (when we are outside). A touch to his butt means go indoors or walk straight ahead. My hand on his back means STOP OR NO, NO! He understands.

Chapter 14 *Sixth Sense*

It is my belief that some dogs are much smarter that people give them credit for. Dogs have a supremacy over Homo sapiens, a sixth sense for sure. They know when you are sad, happy, anxious, mourning, sick, in pain, leaving the house, they sense it all. Some are supernatural.

Casper knows when I am leaving the house before I even get my handbag, car keys or even move his little doggie bed to the laundry room. I have seriously tested various different ways of leaving the house. I will shower before I leave, not shower before I leave, I have thought of everything and physically to nothing to give away the fact that I am leaving but he knows! He will go into the laundry room (where he stays if we leave the house) and he sits and waits! The last thing I do is move his doggie bed from the family room to the laundry room, put up the doggie gate that confines him to the laundry room, give him a doggie treat and leave. But he knows. He's telepathic! It is truly amazing.

Speaking of telepathic last summer my husband had a terrible freak accident at home; he fell and fractured his elbow in three places. He ended up having major surgery and a titanium rod to replace the elbow. When he returned from the hospital I could tell that Casper sensed how much pain he was in. He didn't go near the injured arm, instead he would lie next to my husband and lick and lick the other arm.

The healing process was very long but once the stitches were out and the sutured area was healed Casper would lie and lick only the hand on the injured arm. Not until just recently has he started licking the very spot on the scar area where the actual pain occurs and it just happens to be where the titanium rod is placed. He knows it is still painful possibly senses the foreign object and he wants to help.

Recently Casper has started sensing when my husband has returned home from working all day. If Casper and I are out in our backyard on the swing he will sit up, walk to the edge of the swing and wag his tail. He knows before I do when his Daddy drives into the front driveway.

Casper also knows if a human or canine is on the sidewalk next to our house. If we are outside swinging and he catches a scent he will jump up on the back edge of the swing, wagging his tail.

Casper Chilling'

Chapter 15 *Life Is Good*

It is my belief if we as humans had the character and mood of our canine friends, what a wonderful world it would be! Of course we couldn't go around peeing on trees, tires or the leg of a human (although I must admit there have been times I would have loved to have done so; lift my leg on a human that is)! Definitely we couldn't go around humping in public, but think of your dog or any dog and just how free spirited and happy they are.

Have you ever just watched your dog after he wakes up in the morning? Some dogs are jumping up and down, others play shy! Casper loves mornings! When he wakes he literally jumps up in a complete circle sometimes over and over then crawls to the middle of the bed to play shy. I usually crawl up and kiss him then the tail starts. Wag, wag, wag goes his tail. He is so happy I just know he is thinking, "What a great day this is", "I am happy to be alive" "I love you, (great person of mine), give me a kiss, let's go explore, AARF good morning to the world"! "Thank you God for this new day"! What a beautiful morning it is! I love you, I love you! Belly rubs, belly rubs please!

Casper sleeps in the bed of course. My husband and I are usually the first ones to wake as Casper prefers to sleep in, but if he wakes up and there's no one in bed but himself he will give a loud AARF to let us know he needs to get up and most likely go outside.

Casper will never jump down off of anything. Whether it is eight inches or three feet he will not jump down. I imagine to him it's a great abyss. He has no way of knowing how far it is downward. If he can't touch his foot to it he will just sit and wait.

Casper 5 years old

Chapter 16 *Run Free*

Some may say Casper trained us, maybe so. But whichever way the training went it doesn't really matter to me, because it worked. Casper is very self-sufficient little boy. He can't open doors nor can he ever be let outdoors without being on a leash but no dog should.

Casper's sense of smell and his long white nose are still the most important factors of navigating in his dark world. Currently his sniffer is so good he can smell an unpeeled apple when it's removed from the refrigerator. Casper can smell the neighbor kids next door if they are out in their own back yard or if kids are playing on the sidewalk next to our house. If he is outside with me I can always tell when he has picked up a scent. His nose goes up in the air and he will high tail it to the fence wagging his tail because he smells "kids" through the block wall! Good sense of smell you think? Yes indeed, his smell is extra, extra strength compared to most dogs that are blessed with their sight and good ears.

To date Casper continues to use his paw sign. He's really getting good at it. I tried paw signing to him one day, and it freaked him out! He jumped back as though he was saying "what the heck do you think you're doing speaking paw "!

Casper also has a doggie stroller that was purchased well before he was born for Schnitzel. Later it worked out great for both of them. One could walk and one could ride, or if I wanted to go for a fast walk they both could ride.

I started Casper's walks when he was just a baby but he needed a little more time to adjust to the world before tackling walking on a lease. I started him out slow when he was young but he didn't and still doesn't go for walks like other dogs. There is no straight forward for him it's very confusing as his nose leads him in many directions.

After we moved to the new house I started walking Casper in his stroller down to the green belt of the community that we live in. The big grassy area is as big as a football field. The first walk was a whole new experience for Casper and I. When I took him out of the stroller and let him loose on the grass he ran as free as a bird! He didn't run as fast as a dachshund is capable of but oh was he excited! It was so amazing to watch him. He reminded me of a child taking his first steps or a baby bird taking flight for the first time.

Casper was a little apprehensive at first with no boundaries around him, but once he felt my closeness he was comfortable and took off in a run! He smelled all the scents of everything and everyone that had ever stepped foot on that grass. After just a few minutes he literally slowed to a strut. He did it so very proudly it brought tears to my eyes. What a life changing event it was for him.

We still currently go for walks and when we get about half way to the park area he starts getting antsy and starts to bark as he knows he is going to be put down to run free. He absolutely loves it!

Chapter 17 *Road Block*

You probably wonder what happens if we rearrange furniture indoors or out. We don't! On one occasion, just recently, we did switch a chair and love seat around both into the same spot as the other. The split second he walked into the room he stopped, walked cautiously and sniffed both pieces of furniture and adaptively carried on. We really try not to move things around because comparatively speaking it would be like putting a road block right in the middle of the freeway for us.

Casper continues liking water warm of course. He gets monthly baths and still goes through his frisky ceremony of jumping in circles. Although he doesn't have fountain grass to jump in a fluffy beach towel seems to serve the same purpose for him

As Casper gets older he is has developed the mindset of a small child for sure! When I get busy on the computer, the phone or do anything that the attention is not focused completely on him he finds something to get into.

During this past Christmas season he managed to un-wrap the gifts under the tree while I was on the phone. He has also been known to grab a mouthful of a throw rug I have in front of the kitchen sink, while my husband and I are having dinner. He will shake, shake, and shake it just to get our attention. You're thinking right now he is spoiled? Of course he is and that's his right for getting this far in life! Plus it keeps me active!

Casper's sleeping habits have changed dramatically since he was a baby. For the past 3 years he has become an excellent sleeper. He loves to stretch out and hog the bed. His paws must touch part of our body. He is so secure knowing he is sleeping next his parents. Some day's he sleeps so late and I have to wake him up. He is so cozy in the bed that smells like his people.

Casper was a challenge from infancy up to around the age of two years old; however, did he earn the title of being the Helen Keller of dogs, no not to me or his Daddy. He was a baby who needed to learn by a loving touch and patience and that is exactly what we gave him. Common sense played a little part in his rearing and of course trying to stay consistent which was the hardest part for me personally. As he has grown he has mellowed and knows what he is allowed to do. There really isn't much he isn't allowed to do because he is such a well-mannered little guy.

Chapter 18 *All He Needs Is Love*

This past September we celebrated Casper's 5th birthday. We took him out to dinner (he loves to ride in the car) to a local burger place that has outdoor seating. Casper sat patiently (in one of the chairs at our table) and got bites of our hamburger and fries. Afterwards, we took him to the local ice cream shop, also with outdoor seating and we sat and fed him little bites of ice cream with a sampler spoon (neither is in his regular diet). He was such a good boy. Never "Aarfed" a word and other patrons enjoyed watching him. Happy Birthday, Casper!

At the age 5 years Casper has lived a lot longer than some anticipated. I thank God every day for this blessing. His life has been full of love and TLC and he is truly a very happy and content little fur boy and such a joy to our home.

Recently his Veterinarian advised us that Casper has developed cataracts in both eyes, but he doesn't seem to be experiencing any discomfort. Eye surgery is something we want to avoid forever unless his eyes start to build up pressure. We have been educated on what to watch for in the future and we will have the eye surgery to remove the cataracts if it gets to the point his Vet thinks it's necessary.

Just a few weeks ago we saw a photo of little white and beige dachshund that resembled Casper except she had big beautiful eyes. While talking with our granddaughter in Reno by the of Skype I showed her the picture of what Casper might look like if he had a good pair of eyes. And she replied, "If Casper could see and hear he wouldn't be Casper"! And she is so correct. Casper wouldn't be Casper if he could see and hear. I am guessing his personality would be different and that is one of the sweetest things about him. Casper is Casper because of his disabilities and we wouldn't change one single thing about him. He is an amazing little guy, born into a very dark world and is so happy to be alive.

The day we brought Casper into our home was the day we vowed to give him the best life and the unconditional love that he so deserved. That is exactly what we have done and will continue to do as long as Casper lives. I often ask myself about the label "special needs that I placed on Casper. But I think it is a fair assessment of this "special" little guy and his need is one that is so easy to give, and that is love.

THE END

Visit me on Facebook
Casper T. Armstrong

Made in the USA
Lexington, KY
19 August 2017